Read-About® Geography

Alaska

By Su Tien Wong

Consultant
Nanci R. Vargus, Ed.D.
Assistant Professor of Literacy
University of Indianapolis, Indianapolis, Indiana

Children's Press®
A Division of Scholastic Inc.
New York   Toronto   London   Auckland   Sydney
Mexico City   New Delhi   Hong Kong
Danbury, Connecticut

Designer: Herman Adler Design
Photo Researcher: Caroline Anderson
The photo on the cover shows Bear Glacier at Kenai Fjords National Park.

Library of Congress Cataloging-in-Publication Data

Wong, Su Tien.
    Alaska / by Su Tien Wong.
        p. cm. — (Rookie read-about geography)
Includes index.
Summary: A simple introduction to Alaska, focusing on its regions and their
geographical features.
    ISBN 0-516-22724-6 (lib. bdg.)   0-516-27938-6 (pbk.)
    1. Alaska—Juvenile literature. 2. Alaska—Geography—Juvenile literature.
[1. Alaska.] I. Title. II. Series.
    F904.3.W58 2004
    917.9'8—dc22
                        2003016893

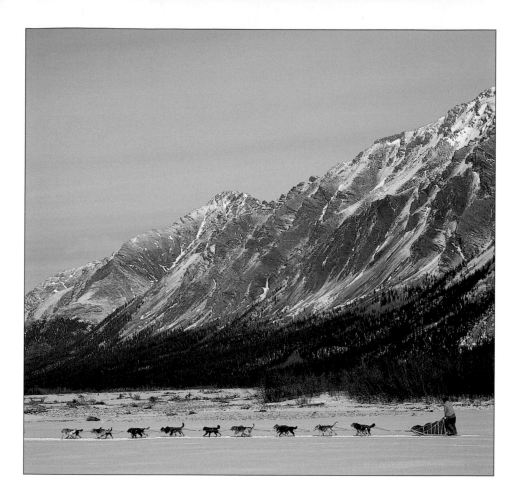

Which state is called "the great land"?

It is Alaska!

Alaska is the biggest
state in the United States.
It is separate from the
other states.

Can you find Alaska on
this map?

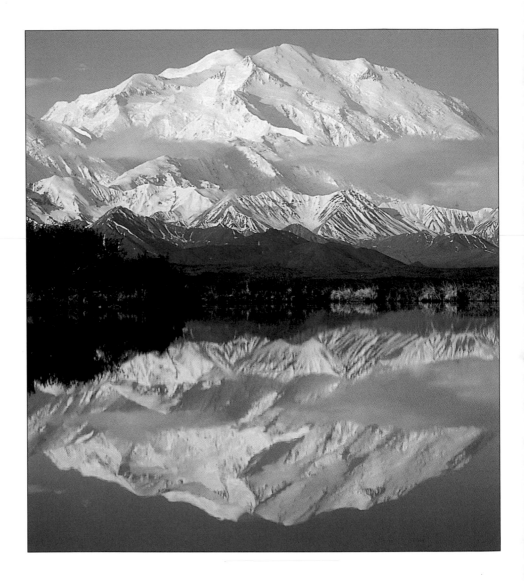

The tallest mountain in North America is in Alaska. It is called Mount McKinley.

The largest glacier (GLAY-shuhr) in North America is in Alaska. It is called Malaspina.

A glacier is a moving mass of ice.

Alaska has many islands, lakes, and rivers. An island is land that has water on all sides.

Kodiak Island is the biggest island in Alaska.

Alaska has long, cold winters and short, cool summers.

The coldest town in the United States is Barrow. Barrow is far to the north in Alaska.

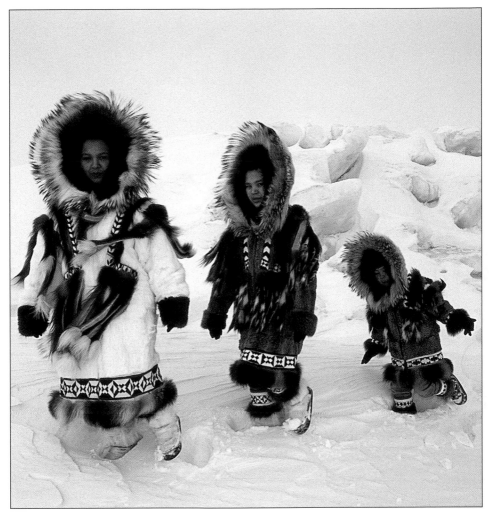

The Inuit people dress in parkas to keep warm.

14

One of Alaska's nicknames is "Land of the Midnight Sun."

From May 10 until August 2, the sun is always out in Barrow.

There are many kinds of animals in Alaska. There are bears, moose, caribou (KAR-ruh-boo), wolves, and birds, too.

Wolf

The state bird is the willow
ptarmigan (TAWR-mih-guhn).

Whale

Whales and dolphins swim
near the coast of Alaska.

Seals, walruses, and sea
otters are found there, too.

Walruses

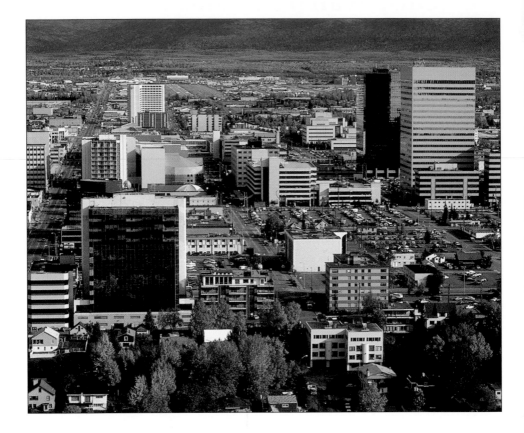

Many people live in or near Anchorage. Anchorage is Alaska's biggest city.

It has tall buildings. There is wildlife there, too.

Some people live in southeastern Alaska. This part of Alaska is shaped like the handle of a pan.

Juneau (JOO-noh) is Alaska's state capital. It is in Alaska's panhandle.

ARCTIC OCEAN

RUSSIA

ALASKA

Fairbanks•

CANADA

Anchorage•

North

West ✦ East

South

Juneau ★

Gulf of
Alaska

SCALE 1 inch = 300 miles

0   Miles   300

0   Kilometers   475

PACIFIC OCEAN

23

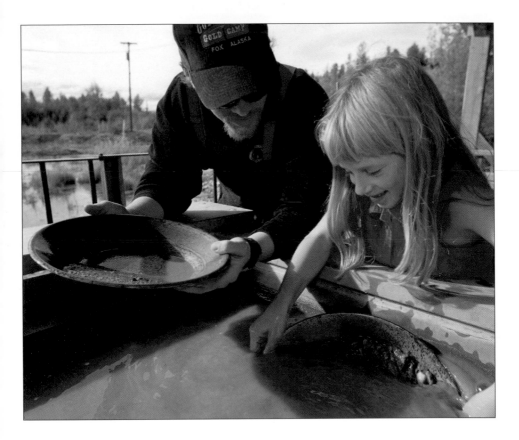

If you move northwest of the panhandle, the winters are cold. The summers are warm.

The main city is Fairbanks. People first came to Fairbanks looking for gold.

Many people in Alaska
are teachers, doctors,
and nurses.

Some fish for a living.
Most work for the
government.

Many people visit Alaska
each year. They come to
see dogsled races, totem
poles, and the beautiful sky.

Totem pole

What would you like to
see in Alaska?

Words You Know

Anchorage

Barrow

Malaspina Glacier

Mount McKinley

totem pole

whale

willow ptarmigan

31

Index

About the Author

Su Tien Wong is an author of children's books. She resides in Westchester County in New York.

Photo Credits

Photographs © 2004: Alaska Division of Tourism: 19 (Nancy Long), 27; Alaska Stock Images: 14, 30 top right (Chris Arend), cover (Michael DeYoung), 24 (Patrick Endres), 29 (Calvin W. Hall), 16 (Tom Soucek); Peter Arnold Inc.: 10 (Joel Bennett), 3 (Kim Heacox), 28, 31 top right (S.J. Krasemann), 17, 31 bottom right (Chlaus Lotscher), 13 (Michael Sewell), 6, 20, 30 top left, 31 top left (Clyde H. Smith), 8, 30 bottom (Jim Wark); Seapics.com/Duncan Murrell: 18, 31 bottom left.

Maps by Bob Italiano